BOA

EDITIONS LTD

THE BOOK OF GOODBYES

ℒℛℯ

WINNER, 2013 ISABELLA GARDNER POETRY AWARD

THE BOOK OF GOODBYES

ഐ

POEMS BY
JILLIAN WEISE

AMERICAN POETS CONTINUUM SERIES, No. 138

BOA EDITIONS, LTD. ഐ ROCHESTER, NY ഐ 2013

First Edition
13 14 15 16 7 6 5 4 3 2 1

For information about permission to reuse any material from this book please contact The Permissions Company at www.permissionscompany.com or e-mail permdude@eclipse.net.

Publications by BOA Editions, Ltd.—a not-for-profit corporation under section 501 (c) (3) of the United States Internal Revenue Code—are made possible with funds from a variety of sources, including public funds from the New York State Council on the Arts, a state agency; the Literature Program of the National Endowment for the Arts; the County of Monroe, NY; the Lannan Foundation for support of the Lannan Translations Selection Series; the Mary S. Mulligan Charitable Trust; the Rochester Area Community Foundation; the Arts & Cultural Council for Greater Rochester; the Steeple-Jack Fund; the Ames-Amzalak Memorial Trust in memory of Henry Ames, Semon Amzalak and Dan Amzalak; and contributions from many individuals nationwide. See Colophon on page 74 for special individual acknowledgments.

ART WORKS.
arts.gov

State of the Arts

NYSCA

Cover Design: Sandy Knight
Cover Art: Matthew Woodson
Interior Design and Composition: Richard Foerster
Manufacturing: McNaughton & Gunn
BOA Logo: Mirko

Library of Congress Cataloging-in-Publication Data

Weise, Jillian Marie.
   [Poems. Selections]
The book of goodbyes : poems / by Jillian Weise. — First edition.
     pages ; cm
   ISBN 978-1-938160-14-1 (pbk) -- ISBN 978-1-938160-15-8 (ebook)
   I. Title.
PS3623.E432474C65 2013
813'.6—dc23
                              2013013139

BOA Editions, Ltd.
250 North Goodman Street, Suite 306
Rochester, NY 14607
www.boaeditions.org
A. Poulin, Jr., Founder (1938–1996)

for Josh Bell, immanentizing the eschaton

CONTENTS

ONE

UP LATE AND LIKEWISE

It never stopped raining when I was with him
and we were wet and there were parties.
He was from another decade. It was honest.

With some you can never tell but with him
I could. My decade let the POWs come home.
What did your decade do? The thing about him is

he keeps being the thing. You could never
count on him. I did. It never stopped raining
and I could, it was honest, tell.

Would you like to be in the same decade with me?
Would you like to be caught dead with me?

THE UGLY LAW

Any person who is diseased, maimed, mutilated or
can I continue reading this? Will it affect my psyche

so that the next time Big Logos comes over
I will not be there in the room? Instead I will be

wandering a Chicago street in my dress with my
parasol as a cane, on the verge of arrest, where arrest

could mean "stopping" or "to keep the mind fixed
on a subject," where the subject is the diseased,

maimed, mutilated self of 19th c. Chicago, the self
in any way deformed so as to be unsightly

and will I tell him to stop looking, tell him I'm tired
and I'm about to be arrested for walking in public

and I can't possibly climax when I am *an improper*
person who is not *allowed in or on the streets,*

highways, thoroughfares or will he say we're alone,
no one is watching, there is your bedside table

and there your mirror and who am I kidding?
I won't tell him anything. There is no room

in bed for this. It does no good to bring things up
from the 19th c. or from last week when the things

have to do with—how do I say it—what is the word
I usually use? Last week I said it like this:

"Big Logos, a moth came out from hiding
as soon as I had taken my leg off and the moth

said, 'Ha little cripple. Now you can't get me
with the broom.'" Then I laughed so he would

know it's okay to laugh. I do it like a joke.
I do it like it's nothing. Why the cover-up?

Why are the laws stacked with it and I never
in high school heard of it? *The maimed shall not*

therein or thereon expose himself or herself
to public view under penalty of staring,

pointing, whispers, aphorisms such as "We are all disabled"
or "What a pretty face you have" or "God gives

and God takes away" or *one dollar for each offense.*
One dollar in 1881 is like $20 today. I wanted to compare it

to something like dinner at Ruby Tuesday or a bra
on sale at Victoria's Secret, as if by comparing

the amount to something I have bought, I would buy
the penalty out. Then the penalty and all its horror

would be gone instead of arrested, kept in mind,
dwelled on when Big Logos comes over or forget him

when I am in the supermarket or forget the supermarket
when I am in front of twenty-four legs in a classroom

or forget the classroom when I am on the couch
watching TV: how will I not think of the woman

in Chicago trying to hide her limp, her thoughts
on her limp, trying not to bring it up, draw attention to it,

or what will happen if she is caught by the constable?
On the conviction of any person for a violation

of this section, if it shall seem proper and just,
the fine provided for may be suspended for 130 years

until a person enters "cripple" in the search engine
on Project Muse because a person has no cripple friends

and has started to think cripples don't exist
and never did and finds the law. Why have I posted

the ordinance on the mirror and why have I traded
the lube in the bedside table for a twenty dollar bill?

What's that supposed to do? Help the history slide in?
Help me remember? *Such a person will be detained*

at the police station, where he shall be well
in the company of criminals, concrete and moths

and a small window to the forbidden street *cared for,*
until he can be committed to the county poor house.

I am not poor. I am not even unsightly. What a pretty face
I have I've been told. Big Logos, will you attest

to my sightliness? Is this all in the past? Why are you
sleeping with me, anyway? Aren't you afraid?

DECENT RECIPE FOR TILAPIA

Tell your back home friends it means nothing
and you will drop him as soon as you have
friends in the city. If you had more friends,

you would not sleep with him. If not him,
who would share your Tilapia? No beloved meal
begins, "Alone before a plate of fish . . ."

Find your market. "Are you single?" the man
behind the counter asks. What to think?
For meals, you are inside a couple.

From inside the couple, you have someone
to call while standing in line. "Does your
girlfriend know?" you must never ask.

Instead, "So many fish and which?"
The laws of attraction are this: There are
no laws of attraction. A person likes

a person. Both parties like each other
and in each other enjoy being liked.
Baste the fish in lemon and butter.

They say it takes time to meet people.
Do you agree? Sleep with your friend.
Disagree? Cut him off. Put it in the oven.

I'VE BEEN WAITING ALL NIGHT

I reckon you were asleep with your girl
before the phone rang. Make something up.

I've been waiting all night to tell you
about the couple in post-War France,

the woman fresh in her grave
and the man who didn't like his mistress dead,

no sir, and so exhumed her, to the dismay
of his wife, who had him arrested

for the stink he made.
She was reburied, returned to the dead.

After jail, he dug her up to fuck again.
Attached suction cups and crafted

a wig from a broom. You can go now.
I'm more in the mood than you're used to.

CAFÉ LOOP

She's had it easy, you know. I knew her
from FSU, back before she was disabled.

I mean she was disabled but she didn't
write like it. Did she talk like it?

Do you know what it is exactly?
She used to wear these long dresses

to cover it up. She had a poem
in *The Atlantic*. Yes, I'll take water.

Me too. With a slice of lemon.
It must be nice to have *The Atlantic*.

Oh, she's had it easy all right.
She should come out and state

the disability. She actually is very
dishonest. I met her once at AWP.

Tiny thing. Limps a little. I mean not
really noticeable. What will you have?

I can't decide. How can she write
like she's writing for the whole group?

I mean really. It's kind of disgusting.
It's kind of offensive. It's kind of

a commodification of the subaltern
identity. Should we have wine?

Let's have something light. It makes
you wonder how she lives with herself.

I wouldn't mind. I would commodify
and run. She's had it easy.

I can't stand political poetry.
She never writes about it critically.

If it really concerns her, she should
just write an article or something.

I heard she's not that smart. My friend
was in class with her and he said

actually she's not that smart.
I believe it. I mean the kind of language

she uses, so simple, elementary.
My friend said she actually believes

her poems have speakers. Oh, that's rich.
I'm sorry but if the book is called

amputee and you're an *amputee*
then you are the speaker.

So New Criticism. Really I don't like
her work at all. I find it lacking.

HOW TO TREAT FLOWERS

Take the flowers directly home. Make no sloppy small talk with women biting into oranges on park benches. Do not leave the flowers in the car, not even if you are the kind of guy who has a sun visor and dark-tinted windows. You must never leave the flowers in the car.

*

If the flowers are carnations—why? Wasn't she worth roses? Wasn't there a summer bouquet with a few sprigs of baby's breath, one or two roses and maybe a lily? You cheapskate. Why are you such a cheapskate?

*

Leave the flowers on the kitchen table, in their clear plastic wrap, beside the blender. She will cut the plastic wrap with her favorite pair of white-handled scissors.

*

You buy the flowers. She cuts the stems, runs water warm, sprinkles sugar in the water, because somewhere, if you heard her correctly, somewhere before you (you forgot there was a *before you*) another man told her to put the flowers in sugar water.

*

None of this will happen in time. C. S. Lewis swears all of time is written on an 8 x 11 piece of paper and the paper is God. You don't believe in God, but . . . If time is written on an 8 x 11 piece of paper, all of time, if that's true, then you are simultaneously buying flowers, taking the woman from the park bench in your mouth and making love to your girlfriend while she watches a stranger pee into your commode. It is, after all, your commode. Where is your rage?

*

I notice you, noticing you, nostalgic for the time before you, which is her time not yours, which you would like for yours, which you would like to pocket along with the change from the ten dollar bill, since the flowers were only five, since you bought carnations, roses were ten, and though you had the ten dollar bill, you wanted something (Spinoza and others agree: "Desire is the essence of man"), a beverage, which requires going into the bar, asking the woman with the orange if she will join you in the bar. Isn't she hot in this heat? She must be.

*

We are getting stale. I call us stale. I can feel us getting stale and it sickens me.

More.

You sicken me.

More.

I took the flowers and I cut the stems off the flowers. I cut the stems off the flowers because you wanted me to do it. You urged me to cut the stems off the flowers and I do not regret one bit of it. Not even in the morning.

*

The problem with flowers and buying them is implicit in the exchange of, yes, that ten dollar bill. Times you have bartered flowers for sex? Times you have tried to barter flowers for sex? People in the world who believe in time? Time it will take for the woman biting into the orange to look up and notice your flowers?

*

Spinoza says, "One and the same thing can at the same time be good, bad and indifferent." The same thing, at the same time, look up, oranges are the essence of man, biting into them is the essence of man, look up, look up. Aren't you hot? In this heat, you must be.

AFFAIRS

Affairs are amply appreciated by contemporary critics under the name of discontinuity. Affairs come into their own when we translate the whole question from structure to behavior. Affairs disappear altogether. Many affairs remain unabsorbed. The concept of the affair gives another dimension to the impact of epiphanies. Affairs in general may be analyzed according to whatever distinctions one uses in analyzing. Affairs are associated with shortness. Final affairs are an obstacle to artistic comprehension caused by the seemingly premature placing of the end. Such affairs exist in every perception that one's tentative comprehension is not complete. Such affairs depend on the convention that "every thing counts." Affairs challenge us at a more fundamental level. Affairs are never completely resolved. Final affairs are the most extreme.

POEM FOR HIS GIRL

I'll tell you which panties
look good on you

psychedelic plaid
with ruffles on the waist

patriotic polka dot
the whale print is very

what's his name again?
Those would look good on you

those too, those also
I could see you

wearing those in his truck
out past the Esso station

to the field party
that one time

you got drunk
and fucked around

with some of his friends
and he cracked 6 beers

and felt old and drove
to the cemetery

and pissed on yr father's grave
here he comes round

the corner—
Are you writing about her?

I hope you're not
writing about her

If we went shopping
I mean today dammit

you could ask why
I'm sleeping with him

then push me
into the hangers

I'm not supposed
to try you on anymore

The dead walk into poems
all the time

Nobody complains

INTERMISSION

TINY AND COURAGEOUS FINCHES

Iguazú Falls, the Argentine side, a cave,
behind the water, two tiny and courageous
finches, Bitto and Marcel, spend the day
flying in and flying out.

Bitto is most proud, daily caw, paid
vacation and space to think aloud.
He likes knowing where everyone is
and that where they are, he is far from.

He keeps his finch friends, outside,
keeps a wife, Lydia, who works domestics.
Marcel comes to the job stoically,
not as proud as Bitto, with not

as many friends. He is big, rigid,
balks at the thought of changing
for anyone, an ounce. He likes to read
the classics, Hesiod, with rules,

everything no nonsense, such as—
"Take precautions, do not dawdle,
have some brains, be honest."
Why were they, from all finches, picked?

Bitto thinks it due to he was a great
rambler once and rambled to Uruguay
and rambled on back. Marcel thinks
it due to he was exiled, he was a great

pain in the ass once, and in front
of the Minister, called Kate a flaccid,
incompetent whore and told her
to get lost in the Arbolis.

This was his way of saying: I love you
little bitch finch. Why must you prune
the tails of others? Bitto and Marcel
live well together. They work out

the kinks, where to poo and how much
privacy to give. Bitto has even grown
a little fond of Marcel, the older,
the literate, the one who says less.

In this Bitto sees the finch he would
like to be. For now Bitto delights the people
who visit the Falls, flies in singing
weeeee flies out singing *wooooo*.

Bitto tried to explain to Lydia
the water, wide blue, the pressure,
the pinch, the wee-woo of it,
the climax, he called it,

which ticked her off and meant
many nights of scavenging
extra tacky shit to nest her with,
a gold thread, a baby's bib.

In return, she lays a good egg.
She lets him do what he wants.
She listens to his day. "Today,
a family of four, Denmark.

The lady took pictures, the man
thought of sneaking away,
the daughter of ice cream, the son
of pillaging, something or other."

Marcel, in a rare breach of silence,
said, "You know why all those photos?"
"The Falls are pretty this time of year?"
"She thinks if she takes enough

and if everyone is smiling and if
she places them on her mantel—"
"What is a mantel?"
"She will not be alone in the world."

Bitto said he liked the idea of a mantel.
Bitto told Lydia he liked the idea
of a mantel, would build her a mantel,
when they grow old in the Arbolis.

Marcel flies the Falls, his left wing
aching, will there be no stop?
He cheeps for the children,
holds his poo and acts happy.

He sees that Bitto is happy
and it irks him because
to be happy requires it seems
some lying and good timing.

So Marcel cracks a seed and works
on his index of every time
a finch appears in print.
He dreams of someday turning

the index into an anthology, which all
finches will read with interest,
thereby validating his work and they
will present him on the mountain,

during the yearly festivities, where
all finches gather. This gathering
arouses in Marcel a sense of place
in the world, an ambition to congregate

with other finches, as long as they
know him by nametag only.
Once Marcel allowed himself
to be known, with Kate, on the mountain.

She asked the basic questions—
How many finches do you flock with?
Do you want to sit on my eggs?
Where do you see yourself in three days?

In the cave, Marcel thinks of Kate,
how she looked perched on the crag
that first afternoon. She liked to read
the surrealists. Her chirping

did not aggrieve him as other chirps did.
While Marcel saw himself as a loner,
a misanthrope, Kate was a weirdo too.
Giving things up, Marcel thought.

He might give things up for Kate.
Bitto did not make such sacrifices.
He kept Lydia in thick leaves.
Bitto believed in what he called

"the spirit of the moment"
which is why Bitto enjoyed
his job genuinely. Except when
the ladies of Brazil entered the cave

like this one, carrying a baby,
dropping it into the Falls.
Next an older man, with cane,
who came almost everyday, his wife

had disappeared. Next a couple
from Australia, where ten years
into a marriage, a stall, an impasse.
The cave was quiet for a while.

Bitto thought about Lydia
and building a mantel.
Bitto continued flying in
and out of the Falls, for no one,

for himself, for the spirit.
Sometimes they talked about God
and did he exist. Bitto said yes,
obviously, faith and feelings.

Marcel said no, obviously, science
and reason. Marcel said,
"I am a spiritual person."
"What is that?" Bitto asked.

"Decency." / "But wait!
Spiritual means a spirit. Do you
have one?" / "Do I think
there's a spirit of Marcel? No."

"Then you're not spiritual."
Marcel let the conversation drop.
His wings hurt from flapping.
He could not be bothered with Bitto's

spirituality, skinny little Bitto.
The closest Marcel came to religion
was when he had to humor Hesiod
who believed in theogony.

Around this time, Kate visited.
"I'm here to deliver a message
from the Minister of Finches,"
Kate said, looking awfully

subdued in her new plumes.
Marcel believed she was not
only there for that reason.
He spent each day sorting

through reasons people came
to the Falls and there was never
only one reason for coming,
there were five or six reasons,

stacked on top of each other,
overlapping each other, contradicting
each other, such that humanity
was a big den of squawk.

Marcel knew Kate must have
asked for the assignment and that
to ask for something was to want it.
"Is there anything you want from me?"

Marcel began, "Is there anything
at all I can give you? I spend
my days flying in and out of the Falls,
which is a testament to my strength,

and though I am not spiritual, I like
the surrealists, and I've tried
to write you to describe my nostalgia
for our time on the mountain but I can't

get it right since I don't think
it is nostalgia. That implies something
of the past, lost forever, and a sadness,
a gravity I don't think worthy of us.

Bitto wants a mantel to fill up
with lies and Bitto doesn't mind
because he lives in the spirit
of the moment, but I want more,

like some guidelines, and to write
the Great Index of Finches, so we
can be happy, and I just said *we*,
which is what I mean, you and me,

so if you've come here as courier
from the Minister of Finches,
and nothing more, then you can go now,
but if you've come for other reasons,

stacked reason upon reason, and if
even one of those reasons
tangentially relates to me, Marcel,
then please, speak."

GO ON HIGH SHIP

The Falls were quiet with Bitto gone
to raise feathers and Kate invisible
on Skype and lone Marcel in the cave.
"I'd rather be a zero than a one,"

Marcel thought, looking up from Euclid's
Optics. The sun set on the lagoon
as the tourists ambled through the park.
Marcel was thinking of the rescue

of a girl from a nearby jungle and how,
to be fetched out of something,
you had to be in something and Marcel
wasn't in anything other than a book.

His screen didn't ring, his job paid in seeds,
he had no credit, no authority. He missed
Kate though he did not admit it, instead
he thought, "Why are ones so strange?

If I chirp once, why do I want, always,
another and am not content until I get it?"
Then he performed an experiment.
CHIRP, sang Marcel and tried to let be,

go on with reading. He couldn't
and before he knew it, CHIRP, CHIRP.
He felt better and looked to Bitto's empty
bed of leaves stolen from trees and wondered

what sort of feathers Bitto was raising.
"He is a liar and a thief," Marcel thought
and knew he was right to think so,
but even lies add up to something.

The Goldfinch sauntered in, half past
six, with briefcase and insurance.
He always talked what-if-something-
happened instead of what-did-happen.

Goldie had these ideas, these grand ideas,
such as "You are only pleased when eating
ice cream," and "In Key West," and etc.
Marcel wished Bitto was there.

Bitto liked to take Goldie's words
and muck them so that Goldie's words
on nothingness became in Bitto's beak—
"Nothing that jizz and nothing that jizzm."

Today, all business. "We should insure
your left wing," Goldie said. "What if
it gives out permanently?" Marcel flapped
the wing to show it worked.

Goldie opened his briefcase, pulled papers
from it and set them on the dirt. "What if
a giant sloth lumbered in and wanted
the cave for himself and used the pages

from your books for toilet paper
and ate you?" "If I'm eaten, what do I
need insurance for?" Marcel said.
After all he was not in anything,

not in trouble, not in a bind, not in
a socioeconomic climate of anxiety,
he was just a finch. "Besides," he said.
"I have never seen a sloth. I'm not sure

sloth exist and suppose they do, what
would an animal of gargantuan size
want with a cave of this size?"
"You never know," Goldie said,

wetting a talon with his tongue.
It was getting late. Marcel wanted
to return to reading Euclid. He knew
what was next: the Grand Ideas

Monologue that Goldie gave and when
he delivered it, he liked his listener
to interrupt him and say, "Go on, high ship."
Goldie began: "I got married, I lived

a long life with a wife who stopped
reading my poems when I was forty as if
I died and my poems with me."
Go on, high ship. "So I traveled

south the country, all became hysterical
to me, *ki-ki-ri-ki, no rou-cou, no rou-cou-cou.*
I was losing my mind, and in losing it,
I realized I had nothing and nothing had me."

Go on, high ship. "I told my biddy,
I don't love you. If I said I loved you
I meant the nothing that is."
Go on, high ship. "I'm in love with

plough-boys and old women in wigs
and bowls and broomsticks and paltry
nudes and dwarfs." Go on, high ship.
"I'm in love with Florida and Havana

and the Carolinas and Hartford,
but mainly Florida." Goldie wet his talons
and bowed his head. Marcel thought
his was an old story and he an old finch.

Since he was so unhappy, Marcel figured
he should do something, become
the what-did finch. But you can't tell
finches what to become.

Later Marcel had difficulty falling asleep.
I will not think dirty things. I will keep
the brain sharp for Euclid, honest for Hesiod.
The cave was cold. Marcel saw the folds

of Kate's plumes near her breast and while
it wasn't dirty, it wasn't clean either,
what he was thinking, and Marcel said, No.
That is all that was, that is what-did.

That is done. He turned his thoughts to
Goldie, poor Goldie, wetting his talons.
The moon shone on the lagoon like
a giant sloth. Marcel fluttered close

to the wall of the cave and fell asleep afraid
and began to have his what-if dreams,
of Kate, of high ships, of twos and threes,
like all what-did finches do.

MARCEL ADDRESSES KATE (AS HE WOULD IF HE COULD)

When the call came for me to join Bitto
behind the damn Falls, did I not challenge
the appointment, did I not appeal to
the High Courts and wait in the dark offices

of tree holes and check the box to describe
myself as too birdbrained? Did I not
beg to stay in the Arbolis with you?
Yet you have not returned to me.

I know, I know I got beaked and fifed
Hesiod into your ear when all you
wanted to do was sleep and sometimes
all you wanted to do was pluck me

and that was, will always be, fine by me.
If I quote the Greats too much, know it's
because I'm afraid of you, yep, yep,
how you puff up your feathers, you know

how you do. I'm talking out loud again
to the can of Brahma, Sage of Seven
Ages, Father of Creation: No, I won't
shut up. I'm talking to Kate.

Also when you entreated me
to buy a machine, a machine to show us
what we look like when we're looking at
a machine, I suffered the wages,

the setup and download to find you,
wearing all your feathers, cheeping
with 36 other finches, none of whom
concern what I have to say here:

I am the original plagiarist.
Yet you have not returned to me.
Daily I withhold from one million
strangers, though they be willing.

I withhold the ability of my
cyber gender and this is a stupid
point I agree. No one wins for withholding.
What else can I say? I'm winging this.

At least when we were speaking in our
deplorable way that was something,
that was some smutcaw we had,
and seduced me you did in manners

unprecedented. If I sleep with
other finches, let us here reference
the words of the Apostle Paul: "I hate
what I do." I don't hate you.

I don't even not like you. I've gone
over the branches and can't find you.
Today the gauchos arrived and they want
me to ride on the brim of their sombreros

to the ranch and maybe I will find me there
a finch who reminds me of you and you
will have returned to me.

TWO

WHY I NO LONGER SKYPE

Skype is on your Mac on the table
next to the Malbec and ashtray,
next to the book that cost 120 pesos,
b/c you had to have *Ulysses*
in English. You're in some town
where your name doesn't exist
and they rename you, so you're
never sure who they're talking to.
The screen rings. It's Big Logos.
He downloaded the thing. First
a garbled voice comes from
the keys then, "Can you hear me?"
By the power of gods in Estonia,
makers of software, haters of fees,
the voice says your name and he's
not anyone, though anyone from
Terre Haute to Rome can Skype you,
he's someone you know or knew.
Which tense to use? Then his face
appears by the folders, the clock,
the Firefox, his face on his body
in his bed 8,000 miles away
and he says, "Give me a hug."
You both grab hold of your machines.
You show your eyeballs to each other,
all impressed with yourselves,
as if your eyeballs have not always
been on your head. "Good to see you,"
he says. "Can you look in my eyes?"
You try but you're always looking off.
It's sad but it feels good like you love
reading *Ulysses* and you love being
alone near the Martial Mountains.
He plays a cover of Bruce Springsteen

by Lucero, and what a rad band.
This is the life. This is your friend,
your friend from way back, though
let's be honest, he was more
than that, and not to trouble you
with facts, he's still more than that.
You're so hot for technology.
This is better than IM. You can't
get enough of his pixels and it must,
please tell me, it *must* add up,
all those hours spent listening
to Lucero, who is okay but,
let's face it, not Springsteen,
and all those hours spent watching
Hulu together and now look at you,
staring at your screen, which is
not ringing, which will not ring.
It has always been just a screen.
You can't blame it for that.

PORTRAIT OF BIG LOGOS

If you're there, I will look at the door
to the motel room and I will be in
my violet dress because violet is one *n*
away from violent like come in,
how was your trip, and if you're there,
I will spend the first ten minutes
ignoring you. I will play Philip Glass
and I will play Busta Rhymes.
It depends on what type of there
you are and what you're there for.
I will read Berryman poems to you,
only Berryman and "I'm hungry,"
you will say and you will keep
being hungry and there is no need
for you to be there to know that.
If you're there, you will have stopped
being you, because being there
in a motel room with me is something
you no longer do, not the you
I know and not the you
you know either and that's
the violence of the whole thing.

ONCE I THOUGHT I WAS GOING TO DIE IN THE DESERT WITHOUT KNOWING WHO I WAS

Joshua Tree, CA—A young professional, Jane Doe,
was raped and murdered at the Cactus Motel
off Twentynine Palms Highway Sunday morning.
Officers responded to the call, made from Room H,
Jane had tried the phone, found
the landline dead, flipped her cell, dialed 9-1-1
again and again, tried the front desk,
wanted to call Big Logos, to whom
she was a mistress, and knowing this was not
her weekend in Verona, and knowing it was
her duty to provide mischief not trouble,
liveliness not near-death, and knowing exactly
who would pick up the phone if she called him,
and knowing the voice on the other end
would say, "Yes? Who is it?" a question
Jane decided was not hers to answer, decidedly
none of her business, he would have to do it,
and so far he was doing it daily, making
arrangements in bars to take his dick out,
for his and her enjoyment, under the table,
until his dick became habit, and he said,
you make my dick happen, which made her
feel like a creator of dick, and she loved it,
and she feared losing it, and made no demands
that he leave his girlfriend, and was unmoved
to tell her, he would have to do that,
it ails me, he said, the ailment Jane attributed
to a mid-life crisis, it was easier to think this
than to ask what was really wrong with him,
or what was really wrong with her,
and so resigning him to his ailment in Verona,

she called instead a friend, a distant,
a friend who knew nothing, not the affair,
not the trip to Joshua Tree, a man by the name
of Clint who worked for Express Trucking,
data entry, third shift, Jane knew he would be
awake playing Guitar Hero, or masturbating
to the Girls Gone Wild DVD she'd encouraged
him to purchase, since when they last spoke,
the girls char-charred in the background,
on TV, and Clint loved them, which is when
she made her recommendation to purchase,
because what else did Clint have to live for?
Clint could do nothing for her.
What did she expect Clint to do for her
in Room H, an auspicious letter, the voiceless
glottal fricative, *had has him his her hers*,
letter of breath, of bare sound, of *hate humanity*
and *hell*. She began making bets with God:
she would not encourage Clint to pornography,
she would stop romancing Big Logos,
she would go to church in the morning,
she would find a saint after service,
she would wear long dresses and call mom.
She couldn't call mom in a moment like this,
to tell her a man, possibly dangerous,
certainly deranged, was standing outside,
breathing heavily, banging hard with his fist,
and had no answer when she spoke to him.
"Yes? Who is it?" she asked, expecting *the owner,
the proprietor, the landlord, the hotel manager,
there's been a fire, an earthquake, a problem
with your credit card.* Then remembering
the man with dirty hands who all day walked
back and forth beside her window, from his room
beside hers to desert, from desert to his room
beside hers, she remembered thinking him
attractive, disheveled, t-shirt, khaki shorts,

she could pin him in a lineup, six two,
she remembered thinking of fucking him,
of what that would be, for he was a businessman
at a Fortune 500 company, drove an Audi,
wore sunglasses with a haircut, he had accounts
manageable, he was en route to Los Angeles,
on the red-eye, the kind of man who fucked
stewardesses in supply closets before selling
a pie chart to Tokyo, how far she got thinking,
earlier in the eve, and now hoping desperately,
scanning the room for defense, that it was not
this man, but that it was the owner of the motel,
and she expected some reply from the door,
since otherwise Jane knew no one in Joshua Tree,
had not been to any of the bars, clubs,
nor karaoke joints that the 911 operator
suggested she may have frequented, *are you sure*
you didn't go out anywhere meet anyone?
and though she told the 911 operator:
"I am positive I met no one tonight I am
going to die please he is banging on the door"
the operator didn't believe her, kept insisting
are you sure are you absolutely sure while she
screamed "WHO THE HELL ARE YOU?"
and thought of him passing her window,
thought of him casing the desert, thought
of how before, when before he was not
a threat, she was going to say to his hands
how dirty, he had been walking the desert,
she could see him, digging out the desert,
as he hassled the door knob, hurried past
the window, he was at the back door now,
she had people to tell she loved them,
she had things left to say, and the operator, *Miss*
what are you doing staying out there alone?

SEMI SEMI DASH

The last time I saw Big Logos he was walking
to the Quantum Physics Store to buy magnets.
He told me his intentions. He was wearing

a jumpsuit with frayed cuffs. I thought the cuffs
got that way from him rubbing them against
his lips but he said they got that way

with age. We had two more blocks to walk.
"Once I do this, what are you going to do?"
he asked. "I wish you wouldn't do it," I said.

Big Logos bought the magnets and a crane
delivered them to his house. After he built
the 900-megahertz superconductor, I couldn't go

to his house anymore because I have all kinds
of metal in my body. I think if you love someone,
you shouldn't do that, build something like that,

on purpose, right in front of them.

POEM FOR HIS EX

So what's up? Where are you these days?
Last I heard you worked at a bakery.
Last I read your poems were lower case

with capital content. I used to like
to read them in the dark. It's weird
you're not his girl anymore.

You were the picture in a snow globe
on his desk that I'd go to, shaking,
when he left the room. That room.

Do you remember it? The Dr. Seuss
sheets read: "This is not good.
This is not right. My feet stick out

of bed all night." We tried not to talk
about you. When we had to do it,
I made him go to a dyke bar

so everyone would be on my side.
In my mind you were so good
at everything, like walking.

I asked him if you had two legs.
What was I thinking? Of course
you have two legs. I asked him,

I guess, so that the possibility
of me would exist. He said yes
as if he was ashamed to admit it.

Does it make you feel better
to know he cheated with a handicapped
girl? I wonder if you have

any handicapped friends.
I don't know why I'm using that word.
It demoralizes me. Or if you don't.

Or if you've seen somewhere,
maybe in the bakery, a woman
with a limp and felt sorry.

Once in the dyke bar he said
he was waiting for you to
stand on your own two feet

and it was hilarious to me,
though it was a serious conversation,
so I could not laugh.

We never talk about you now.
It's not allowed. We have to act all
that-never-happened.

I always liked you and thought
you were cool
and sometimes I pretend

you're in the room
and you forgive me and say
you always knew.

GOODBYES

begin long before you hear them
and gain speed and come out of
the same place as other words.
They should have their own
place to come from, the elbow
perhaps, since elbows look
funny and never weep. Why
are you proud of me? I said
goodbye to you forty times.
I see your point. That is
an achievement unto itself.
My mom wants me to write
a goodbye poem. It should fit
inside a card and use the phrase,
"You are one powerful lady."
There is nothing powerful
about me though you might
think so from the way I spit.
I don't want to say goodbye
to you anymore. I heard
the first wave was an accident.
It happened in the Cave
of the Hands in Santa Cruz.
They were drinking and someone
killed a wild boar and someone
said, "Hey look, I put my hand
in it." Saying goodbye is like that.
You put your hand in it and then
you take your hand back.

FOR BIG LOGOS, IN HOPES HE WILL WRITE POEMS AGAIN

Maybe it's because you're cut off
from your roots, and you need to go
to Spain, be with your forefathers,
the Diego Logos, whose remains lie

in the sea surrounding Majorca.
There you'd feel more *insula maior*,
less *insula flatbrain*. There you'd rest
in a hammock, mid-afternoon, writing.

Except such peace makes awful poetry.
There would appear a beetle
by the ill-begotten name of Hydraboo.
He is angry, scaled, with pokey things

like fingers if fingers were shiny blades
of poison. He is evolved beyond
our Horatian notion of beetles. He sees
your left ear and it tenders him,

calms him the fuck down. I can't
blame him for that. Your ear, lined
as it is, like the marks he made by the sea,
and it is soft, with a secret spot

for getting into. Don't you think
he had a day of flat brain?
You bet. But not this day, the day
you swing in the hammock, composing

a much too peaceful crown of sonnets
or just a crown inside a sonnet
or just a curtal sonnet about a king
who lost his ending, an ending who lost

her king, when suddenly beside you
Hydraboo the Beetle wants in your ear.
What will you do? You are a monist.
Bisabuelo Logos was a monist.

Indeed you are a monad. Sometimes
this is what I do when I am especially
missing you: I pretend you are hiding
behind everyone in the world's face

and I have to say the code to reveal you.
This is why I buy so much fruit
from so many different vendors.
I guess I'm on the island too.

Do you mind? I wonder how I got here.
I must've taken a whale.
I say to the vendors, "You are a royal
pumpkin. You are a five-dollar chicken.

Are you not?" No, he is not, and he is not,
and neither is he. On I walk, eating
pomegranates and berries. As Diego
Logos used to say, *Esperanza mis niños,*

and as he spoke he saw Hydraboo,
back when he was half-a-pint,
half-a-toothpick, flat without brain,
pinch without body, scuttle here,

scuttle there. Diego watched him
with your very own eyes before they
were your eyes, when they were still
Diego's eyes watching Hydraboo,

who was not yet boo, and not yet beetle,
more like *be*, only an inkling, before
poems happened, when all writing
was wish and whizgig in sand.

BE NOT FAR FROM ME

He called her number, after many months,
and reached a man named Pete. "This is Pete,"
the man said. "Don't nobody answer here
but me." So she had changed her number.
It was almost like she wanted him to suffer.
It was almost like having her new number
would give him something that belonged
to him anyway. During other hours of the day,
he didn't want her new number and would
content himself without it, until he got drunk,
and thinking, and online found her faculty page.
She never should have said where she worked
if she didn't want him to call her at work.
He dialed and a mechanical voice said, "We
are not available. Please leave a message."
What college had such primitive devices
as standard answering machines? Where
was she? Furthermore, what was this *we*
bullshit? Did the voice know something?
Was she seeing someone? It was just like
leaving any other message except his heart
beat differently. Had it always? Why yes,
hello, you are no longer at the number I had
for you. I spoke to some guy named Pete.
It has been a while but I still miss you.
This is pointless. Once he left the first
message, it was easier to leave the second,
third and fourth. He made a regular habit
of calling her. It was like they talked.
He told her about his student who, by
his recommendation, won the Duquesne
Fellowship. He told her about his reading,
in the Lower East Village, the audience
loved his poetry. He told her about his colleague

who farted, regularly, in the office. It was
always the same. "We are not available.
Please leave a message." The voice was firm.
The voice forced him to leave messages.
He told her about his mom who sent
an Advent calendar with windows full
of Xanax. He told her his mom always said
he was a good eater. He told her to call
and gave his number, though he knew she had it.
Where do you get off changing your number
and not giving me the new one? Not reading
Endless Love by Scott Spencer? Not taking
me up on any of my recommendations
like when I recommend you call me back?
He kept waiting for the tape on the machine
to run out. Every time he called, tenth,
eleventh, and twelfth now, he waited for
the tape to run out. Weeks passed. He took
a Xanax. He drank a beer. It was raining.
There was a song. Someone said something.
He didn't put it that way on the machine.
He didn't say I'm stoned I'm shitfaced
I'm calling because they were playing James
Blunt in the Whole Foods Market. Instead
he told her about the view from his office.
The tops of roofs. The smoke plumes.
The clouds. He was Li Po sometimes
and Catullus others. He made sure to get
sweet after he got vulgar. It must have been
an independent machine, sitting next to
the phone, on her desk in her office.
So he was on her desk talking. This isn't
very nice. It isn't very nice of you to go
away and not tell me how to reach you.
I'm starting to doubt the whole enterprise.
He told her about a podcast and a movie.
Once, after reading Wittgenstein, he left

a message of silence punctuated by
a nipple clamp. Sweet again. Thursday.
It's me. You check this machine. You and me
both know it. The tape never runs out.
Don't ask any questions of me. Stay on
your side of the tape. We're fucked.
I don't love you. I'm sleeping with various
women from the boroughs, professional
and amateur. I miss you. Come see me.
I saw a therapist. Her voice was like a cartoon.
She wore pantyhose with tennis shoes.
I said this is the deal. I'm beginning
to doubt the whole enterprise. There is
no one I've seen that you need know about.
I had a bad dream last night. We died
and came back to find each other in the
Dulles airport bar. That is why it won't
go away. You took me to the Great
Sadness. You look cute even when
emaciated. We were going to survive.
We fully intended to be survivors.
All our poems went up in smoke. Us too.
I'm not writing. I haven't written since
I saw you. I can't write. The therapist
wasn't too worried about it. I couldn't
take her seriously. I lied continuously.
Pick up the phone. You must be checking
your machine. Your students wonder
where you are. Your boss left word.
Don't you have appointments to keep?
Stop erasing me. Keep this one at least.
This is a good one.

CURTAIN CALL

ELEGY FOR ZAHRA BAKER

Zahra Baker is missing. "I don't know. You all know more than I know," says her father. The news on five websites tells the story the same clausal way. A girl, who wears hearing aids and a prosthetic leg, went missing.

Why bring Lacan into it?

I dated this guy who liked to make unannounced visits. "Whaddya know," he would say. "I was just in the area." When we broke up, he said, "You must have had childhood trauma."

I called my mom. "Did I have childhood trauma?"

Where is Zahra Baker's mom?

Zahra Baker was born in 2000. Her parents divorced in 2001. No one can find her mom. They are both missing.

Wednesday. Poetry Workshop. Here I am again talking without thinking. "I have a fake leg and I saw this clip on the news about Zahra Baker who may be dead with a fake leg and it didn't make me cry. It's very hard to make someone cry in poems or on the news."

After I said the words *fake leg*, everyone in the class looked at my feet.

I do not have bone cancer or anything that easy. People know what bone cancer means. She was ten years old. And, if she is still alive, she is still ten years old.

"Zahra was last seen in her bed at 2:30 a.m. on Saturday morning according to her stepmother." —Fox News

"I am gothic and proud." —Stepmother's MySpace page.

"Mr. Coffey, you like being in control now who is in control we have your daughter no cops." —Ransom Note

Her leg was found in the woods. They matched the serial number from leg to medical records. This is how it begins. Serial numbers on our parts. Only our doctors can tell you who we are.

What am I doing with my life?

The commercial starts with a celebrity. The celebrity turns into a potbellied man with a missing leg surrounded by empty beer bottles. "Be thee amputated, drunk and alone? Play Rock Star."

In the spring issue of *Pony Swoon*, Nadine Neeze has a poem titled "Lame Sonnet." Hugh sent the issue. What am I going to do about it? Tell Hugh the word *lame* is offensive? Do I actually care or is this another of my baseless campaigns?

"You used the word lame on the phone the other day," Josh says. "Sometimes I use it just to see how it makes me feel," I say.

In regards to the song "Pretty Boy Swag" by Soulja Boy: It is about a lame boy who goes to the club and because of his limp, which is called "swag," all the women want him.

I am watching *Pawn Stars*. It is about how much something is worth.

How much would you pay me to say the name of the condition I have? Would I just need to say the name or would you require an examination? How much for the box of legs in the attic?

I start calling myself a cyborg.

I find a website called *Gimps Gone Wild*. "I could make a lot of money selling photo sets," I tell Josh. "Probably a hundred dollars for a set."

"Don't do that," he says. "I would never do that," I say even though I'm not sure if I would do it or not.

"Have you seen the Suicide Girls?" I ask Josh. He says, "No. What's that?" It seems impossible that he has not seen the Suicide Girls. "It's porn but the girls are really different with tattoos, librarian glasses, emo, indie, that kind of thing. If the girls on *Gimps Gone Wild* were pretty like the Suicide Girls then maybe."

What is pretty?

I read the novel *Fay* by Larry Brown. I read it fast and pretend Fay has a fake leg. This is a recurring approach I take.

Zahra Baker's stepmother has been arrested for 1) assault with a deadly weapon 2) failure to return rental property 3) writing worthless checks and 4) some other charges not reported. Her father has been released after posting bond.

In the Netherlands, if you are disabled, the government gives you 12 free sessions with a prostitute each year. "For women too?" Josh asks.

A man at a coffee shop. I thought he had a condition that caused him to shake uncontrollably. Later, the emails roll in. "I got turned-on seeing you walk to the stage. I bought your book. Do you like making love?"

The emails got so bad I had to forward them to my professor. He would read them and let me know if I needed a restraining order. Or a gun.

If I enrolled on *Gimps Gone Wild*, I would wear a wig. I would dress up in a ball gown. Employ various speakers. Is it any different than poetry?

Zahra: Here's the drill. There have been so many laws against us. Laws that say we can't go out in public and we can't marry. Laws that mandate the splicing of our wombs and parts of our brains. I was going to lay it out for you in poetry, all the laws against us, but there were just too many.

On the cover of the book Josh is reading: BEST BLACK WRITER. Josh says, "Bet that pisses him off."

Zahra Baker is still missing. I better write some more notes to her before she's dead.

It is weird that I have all these legs in the attic but they would not let me keep the real leg. The real leg they cut off and I guess it went somewhere like to a shelf or an incinerator. Sometimes I wish it had a proper burial.

"Probably has to do with medical waste," Josh says. "There must be laws."

Yesterday was fine. I was straightforward with them. I told them why I wrote the things I wrote. I read with a Native American poet.

Someone asked, "Do you feel the burden of your identities?" I said yeah, I feel it. The Native American said he doesn't think of it as a burden. His first language was Cherokee. He doesn't speak it anymore.

I am writing my acceptance speech for the Best Disabled Writer Award. The speech begins: I need some new words.

Tell us. How is it getting around? It's awful. You have to negotiate with so many people on the sidewalks and you can hear their thoughts, like "Hurry up" and "Why are you walking so slow?" and "Move out of my way."

Zahra: You'll get better at passing. It's a pain in the ass, I know. You'll learn, I promise. Just make it out of the woods.

NOTES

"The Ugly Law": Italicized text comes from an 1881 municipal ordinance, as cited in Susan M. Schweik's *The Ugly Laws: Disability in Public* (NYU Press). Chicago was the last city to repeal its Ugly Law in 1974.

"How to Treat Flowers" quotes Spinoza's *Ethics*, Part III, Prop. 59, as translated by Edwin Curley (Penguin Classics), and draws on C. S. Lewis' chapter "Time and Beyond Time" from *Mere Christianity* (HarperCollins).

"Affairs": This is a substitution poem based on Austin Wright's "Recalcitrance in the Short Story," from the anthology *Short Story Theory at a Crossroads*, edited by Susan Lohafer (LSU Press). "Affairs" has been substituted for "recalcitrance."

"Go On High Ship": Geoffrey Grigson named Wallace Stevens "The Stuffed Goldfinch" for an eponymous review in *New Verse*.

"Elegy for Zahra Baker" engages with the case of Zahra Baker whose remains were found scattered across Caldwell County, North Carolina, in 2010.

ACKNOWLEDGMENTS

Thanks to the editors of these journals where the poems first appeared:

Badlands: "Poem for His Girl";
Cave Wall: "Go On High Ship";
Dossier: "Be Not Far From Me";
Failbetter: "How to Treat Flowers";
Fairy Tale Review: "Elegy for Zahra Baker";
Forklift, Ohio: "Tiny and Courageous Finches";
LIT: "Goodbyes";
Mayday: "Marcel Addresses Kate";
Michigan Quarterly Review: "Up Late and Likewise";
The Missouri Review: "Once I thought I was going to die in the desert without knowing who I was" and "For Big Logos, in Hopes He Will Write Poems Again";
New Ohio Review: "The Ugly Law";
Pax Americana: "Affairs" and "Decent Recipe for Tilapia";
PEN American Poetry Series: "Poem for His Ex";
Pleiades: "I've Been Waiting All Night";
Tin House: "Semi Semi Dash";
Wordgathering: "Café Loop".

Thanks to Peter Conners, Laure-Anne Bosselaar, and Michael Blumenthal, to the ghost of Isabella Gardner, and to the BOA staff. Thanks to the Fulbright Program, the Universidad de Buenos Aires, and Delfina Muschietti for the fellowship and friendship. Thanks to Ana Lopez at the Patagonia Spanish School for making Ushuaia a less lonely place to live. Thanks to Clemson University, the Fine Arts Work Center, and the University of Cincinnati for grants and residencies to support these poems.

Thanks to these writers for their insights on the manuscript: Tom Bissell, Sarah Blackman, Don Bogen, Jim Cummins, John Drury, Tim Earley, Okla Elliott, Michael Griffith, Joanie Mackowski, Kristi Maxwell, Bo McGuire, Catherine Paul, Michelle Santamaria, Craig Morgan Teicher, Gary Weissman, and Thomas Yagoda. Much love for my parents, Doug and Donna Weise.

ABOUT THE AUTHOR

Jillian Weise is the author of *The Amputee's Guide to Sex*, *The Colony*, and *The Book of Goodbyes*, winner of the 2013 Isabella Gardner Poetry Award. Her work has appeared in *The Atlantic*, *The New York Times*, and *Tin House*. Weise has received fellowships from the Fine Arts Work Center in Provincetown, the Fulbright Program, the Sewanee Writers Conference, and the University of North Carolina at Greensboro. She is an Assistant Professor at Clemson University.

BOA EDITIONS, LTD.
AMERICAN POETS CONTINUUM SERIES

COLOPHON

The Isabella Gardner Poetry Award is given biennially to a poet in mid-career with a new book of exceptional merit. Poet, actress, and associate editor of *Poetry* magazine, Isabella Gardner (1915–1981) published five celebrated collections of poetry, was three times nominated for the National Book Award, and was the first recipient of the New York State Walt Whitman Citation of Merit for Poetry. She championed the work of young and gifted poets, helping many of them to find publication.

The publication of this book is made possible, in part, by the special support of the following individuals:

Anonymous
Nin Andrews
Angela Bonazinga & Catherine Lewis
Bernadette Catalana
Anne Germanacos
Melissa Hall & Joe Torre
Robert & Willy Hursh
Keith Kearney & Debby McLean, *in memory of Peter Hursh*
X. J. & Dorothy M. Kennedy
Jack & Gail Langerak
Katy Lederer
Barbara & John Lovenheim
Gert Niers
Boo Poulin
Steven O. Russell & Phyllis Rifkin-Russell

୨ର୍ଜ